Introduction And

What are Clematis?

Clematis are plants of the botanical family Ranunculaceae which also includes other familiar garden plants such as peonies and delphiniums. The majority of cultivated clematis are climbers but a few, notably *Clematis integrifolia* and *C. davidiana* are herbaceous and can be grown among other perennials in the garden border. The word clematis can be pronounced in two ways, klem-a-tis or klem-ay-tis; both are in common use but many horticultural experts prefer the former.

There are several hundred species of clematis and they are found growing round the world from Europe, Asia, America to Australasia. The majority of species and hybrids in cultivation are very hardy but a few, particularly the evergreen species need a very sheltered position outdoors or glasshouse protection to survive.

Garden clematis are often divided into three groups according to the flowering period. Note that the first two groups either flower directly from buds or short stems produced on old wood from the previous season, but the third group flower from midsummer onwards on stems that have grown the same year. This distinction is very important as it largely dictates when the plants should be pruned.

Group One

These consist of early flowering species and their hybrids such as *C. alpina*, *C. macropetala* and *C. montana*.

Group Two

The most typical members of this group are the large flowered cultivars (cultivated varieties) such as the popular 'Nelly Moser'.

Group Three

This is dominated by C. 'Jackmanii' and its relatives but also includes other beautiful species such as *C. orientalis, tangutica* etc and the herbaceous types mentioned earlier.

The different species and hybrids produce flowers of all the normal plant colours but there is, as yet, not a good deep yellow large flowered hybrid although the colour is well represented in the species. Many of the colours change very markedly during the life span of each individual flower, particularly when grown in full sun, and many of the more delicate colours are more enduring if the plants are given a north facing situation. After the flowers have gone the seed heads can be of great ornamental value and they are highly prized by flower arrangers. *C. tangutica, C. orientalis, C. flammula* and *C. fargesii* produce highly ornamental seedheads in great profusion.

Some clematis flowers are scented and *C. montana* 'Elizabeth' is perhaps one of the best for this purpose. Although not the most strongly perfumed it is very vigorous and a large plant can produce thousands of pale pink flowers that fill the air with fragrance. Other worthwhile scented plants include the almond scented *C. flammula* and the vanilla scented *C. montana* 'Wilsonii' and *C. rehderiana* which smells like cowslips. 'Fair Rosamund' is one of the few large flowered hybrids that is noticeably fragrant.

Many clematis cultivars have double flowers but they will also produce single flowers on young plants or when flowers appear outside the normal flowering period. On early flowering types, double flowers are usually produced on the previous seasons wood and single flowers appear later on the current seasons growth. However cultivars such as 'Louise Rowe' can produce both double and single flowers at the same time.

Clematis have a multitude of uses and can be trained over an arch or up and along a wall. They can be used to grow through other trees and shrubs complementing the host with a spectacular display of flowers. The stronger growing species and cultivars of *C. montana* are often used to hide ugly or unsightly buildings or to cover dead tree stumps or bare trunks.

Clematis are undoubtedly the aristocrat of climbers and their unsurpassed range of colour, form and flowering period should guarantee their inclusion in even the smallest garden.

Figure 1.
Parts of a Clematis.

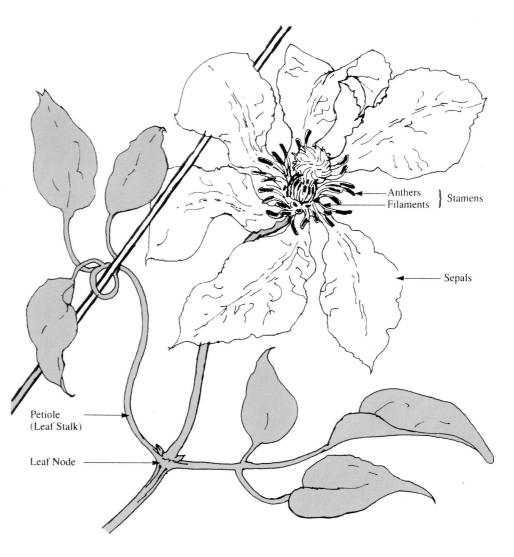

Anthers } Stamens
Filaments }

Sepals

Petiole
(Leaf Stalk)

Leaf Node

Cultivation of Clematis

Planting Position and Aspect

Clematis have a preference for a cool moist root run and thorough preparation of the planting site is more important than for many other less deeply rooting subjects. Needless to say it is sites that have not been deeply cultivated in the past that benefit most from being properly prepared. If the pot is removed from a container grown plant, the worm like roots will be found winding round and round the bottom of the soilball, showing little or no inclination to fill the upper layers. Their main need is to penetrate deeply downwards to find the cool, constantly moist conditions that they prefer. These observations mainly apply to the root systems of the large flowered hybrids, many of the species and closely related small flowered hybrids have a more normal, fibrous root system, but like all plants these will also grow more strongly in well cultivated soil. For this reason, if a chosen planting site has only a shallow depth of soil, the fibrous rooted types will establish themselves more easily than the majority of the large flowered hybrids. Heavy annual mulching with layers of peat or manure will greatly help plants growing in shallow soils.

Planting aspect is another important feature that must not be overlooked. It often dictates how much light the plant will receive and can have an important bearing on the moisture content of the soil. Many clematis such as *C. alpina, macropetala, montana,* 'Henryi', 'Comtesse de Bouchaud' etc. will grow happily facing north as will hybrids like 'Nelly Moser' and 'Wada's Primrose' whose flower colours are prone to fade in sunnier positions. Some of the late flowering species and the more tender types will need to face south or west to take advantage of the extra warmth that such a situation provides. Full details of the needs of each species or cultivar are given in the descriptive sections starting on p.10.

Most types of soils will suit clematis but very sandy and shallow chalky soils tend to dry out rapidly and heavy mulching or frequent watering will be required in dry weather. Similarly, situations close to south facing walls, large trees, shrubs or hedges (particularly privet) should be avoided as these will also be dry. Clematis that are required to cover or grow through a shrub or tree should be planted on the north (shaded) side well away from the trunk, outside the overhang of the branches. The young clematis will not succeed if its roots are forced to compete with another large, well established plant, see the diagram on this page. A supporting bamboo cane or wire can be used to lead new growth towards its host; this can be removed after a few years when the stems of the clematis have thickened sufficiently.

Most Clematis bought from nurseries or garden centres are container grown and providing that the weather is not freezing and the soil conditions are suitable they can be planted at any time of the year. However early autumn or late spring is the best planting time and losses should then be minimal. Summer planting of pot grown specimens will be successful providing that the plants are very well watered during dry weather. Winter planting is best avoided as even some of the strongest and most vigorous plants can succumb when planted in cold, heavy soils.

Figure 2.
Planting.

A hole should be dug at least 18in (45cm) square and deep and if the area is on clay, a little peat and sand should be worked into the bottom of the hole with a fork. Unless the soil is very good only the topsoil should be returned to the hole and the subsoil spread thinly over another part of the garden. The hole is then completely filled using topsoil or John Innes potting compost and firmed by treading it down lightly. A planting hole is then dug in the prepared area to suit the size of the rootball and should be deep enough to allow two to three inches of the stem to be buried below

A hole should be prepared about 45cm (18 ins) square and deep, at least 30cms (12 ins) away from a wall and outside the overhang of any branches. The hole is filled with topsoil or soil based potting compost and the young clematis planted with about 5 to 8 cm (2 to 3 ins) of stem below ground level. Keep the plant well watered until fully established.

soil level. In this way several live buds will be protected and even if the plant is broken or eaten by animals it will be able to regrow. It is also helpful in protecting the plant against a fatal attack of clematis wilt. See the section 'Pests & Diseases'. A little bonemeal worked into the soil at planting time helps the plant to establish a good root system. Sometimes it is recommended to tease apart or slightly loosen the roots before planting, but this can cause damage and it is safer to leave the rootball undisturbed.

A newly planted clematis must be given some initial support. Leave the original cane in position and insert a new one close to, but not through the old soilball, and leading to the wall, pergola, tree stump etc. that it is intended to cover. It is also a good idea, and in many instances essential, to protect the lower 30cm (12in) against the ravages of animals such as rabbits or deer. This can be accomplished with a cylinder of wire netting, the lower end of which is buried a few centimetres (2in) into the soil.

Pruning

In the first spring after planting, all large flowered clematis, including the early flowering types, should be pruned back to the lowest pair of strong buds. This will ensure a bushy framework and be the basis

for a much more attractive plant in the future. A gardener looking forward to the earliest flowers may have difficulty in accepting this advice but in most instances regrowth will be stimulated and the plant will grow away much more strongly than if left unpruned.

In the following years it is essential that the late flowering hybrids such as the 'Jackmanii' types are pruned down to the lowest two or three strongest buds on each stem. These plants produce their flowers on the growth made in that year and if left unpruned will look very untidy. The early flowering hybrids typified by 'Nelly Moser' should not be given this treatment or flowering will be impaired as their flowers develop on the wood produced in the previous season. Pruning should be confined to tidying up the plant by removing unsightly or dead growth immediately after flowering or in February when the young flower or growth buds start to move. Many plants of this type can be left unpruned for several seasons when feeding will be the only maintenance required.

Similarly, vigorous species such as *C. montana* and its hybrids should only have dead or diseased wood removed. However if a plant of this type has become too large, severe pruning will not harm it, but a seasons flowers may be lost.

Figure 4.
Pruning a New Plant.

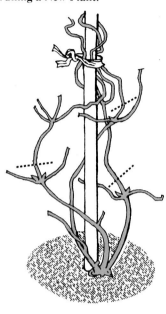

The first February after planting it is important that all types of clematis should have each stem pruned back to the lowest 1 or 2 buds on each stem, normally 15 to 23cm (6 to 9 ins) from ground level.

Figure 5.
Pruning Late Flowering Types.

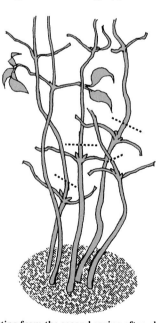

Starting from the second spring after planting the stems of all clematis that start flowering in July or later should be pruned back hard each February to the lowest 2 or 3 buds. Early flowering types should only have nuisance or dead wood removed.

Figure 3.
Protection of Young Plants.

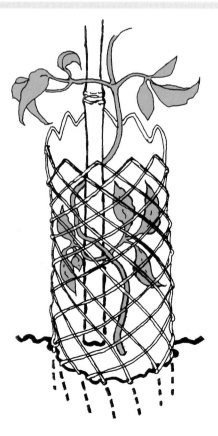

Rabbits and other animals find young clematis shoots very tasty and the plants may need protection by enclosing the lower 30cm (12 ins) in a cylinder of wire netting.

Cultivation of Clematis
Continued

Supports And Training

Clematis will not cling to or damage smooth surfaces such as walls. They attach themselves by twisting their petioles (leaf stalks) around a support so that it is necessary to provide a wire framework or trellis for them to climb up. Masonry nails can be driven into the wall at 23cm (9in) intervals around the edge of a square or rectangle. See figure 6. Do not drive the nails directly into the bricks as this causes damage that cannot easily be repaired but rather place them into the mortar between the bricks. The wires are then strung from nail to nail in the manner shown forming a framework of 23cm (9in) squares. The framework should not lie directly against the wall but be approximately 1 to 2.5cm (1/2 to 1in) away from its surface to allow room for the leaves to twist themselves around it. Plastic coated wire is preferable for the purpose as in sunshine ordinary wire can get very hot. Alternatively trellis can be fixed against a wall using masonry nails or screws and plugs. As the plant grows tie in some of the main stems so that they cover the support evenly; subsequently the plant can be allowed to grow and flower at will.

Clematis can also be used to grow over or among other plants, trees or shrubs. Even dead trees or stumps can be can be utilised to provide support for a clematis. If the area to be covered is large, one of the more vigorous clematis such as *C. montana grandiflora* can be used as it can clamber up 9 metres (30ft) or more and provide a spectacular display. In this situation there is probably room to plant another cultivar, such as 'Victoria' so that a range of flowering periods can be encompassed and what would otherwise be an eyesore can be a mass of changing flower and colour from spring until autumn. However do not plant clematis closer than 1.5m (5ft) to each other.

Many trees and shrubs have only a brief period of spectacular display and a clematis growing through them can enhance them at an otherwise unproductive time. Good examples of such associations include summer flowering clematis growing through Wistaria, Forsythia, Akebia, Kolkwitzia, Rhododendrons, ivy, honeysuckle, virginia creeper, climbing roses etc; the combinations are only limited by the ingenuity of the gardener. Some clematis such as *C. montana* 'Elizabeth' are also recommended for growing through conifers and they certainly give a very spectacular display. However part of the attraction and beauty of certain conifers is associated with their symmetry and clean, smooth outlines and to some eyes the intrusion and overgrowth by other plants spoils the overall aesthetic effect. This decision, based on personal taste, can only be made by each individual grower.

C. integrifolia can be grown in the garden borders along with other herbaceous plants but the climbing types can also be used in these situations as ground cover or to scrabble over the surface until they reach a judiciously placed log, rock or other support where they can ascend giving height and background to the display. Plants suitable for ground cover include *C. montana, alpina, macropetala, orientalis* and *tangutica.* all of which can cover up to 5 to 10 square metres if planted in good soil.

One of the classic positions for growing clematis is over archways, fences and pergolas. With careful choice of cultivars it is possible to have a continuous display of colour from early spring to late autumn. An advantage to planting clematis is that it does not preclude growing other subjects such a climbing roses or laburnum etc. They will grow together in harmony, extend the flowering season and give extra variety and interest with minimal additional effort. Many large gardens have arched doorways leading through brick walls and it is quite common to see a clematis covering the archway and a large part of the wall itself. It is a tribute to the versatility of the clematis that it is suitable for growing not only in stately homes but in the smallest garden or trained around the front door of even the most humble dwelling.

Clematis can be grown successfully for many years in large pots although they live longer and are less trouble to maintain when grown in the open ground. Obviously the more vigorous and rampant growers such as *C. montana, flammula, orientalis* and *tangutica* etc. will quickly outgrow even the largest pot and should be avoided for this purpose.

Figure 6.
Wire Support for Clematis.

Clematis growing against a wall need a support to climb on. A trellis can be used, or a wire framework of 23cm (9in) squares can be constructed with the aid of suitable masonry nails driven into the mortar between the bricks.

The container must be of adequate size, at least 30cm. (12 in.) in diameter and preferably 45cm. (18in.) deep. The depth of the pot is vital to satisfy the need for the roots to penetrate deeply into the soil. The size given above is a basic minimum and a larger container would be an advantage, if only to get the necessary depth. Obviously the plant will be in this container for a long period and it is not possible to repot the plant after it has become established. In these circumstances it is better to use a soil-based potting compost for planting rather than one of the soilless (usually peat based) types; John Innes Potting Compost No.3 being most suitable for the purpose. Planting is carried out in the usual manner but ensure that a layer of crocks is placed in the bottom of the pot to facilitate good drainage. Always keep container grown clematis well watered as they are intolerant of becoming dry at the roots.

Feeding

Clematis are quite hungry plants and even if they have been planted in fertile soil they will benefit from annual feeding. Flowers that gradually become fewer in number or smaller in size are signs that the soil is becoming impoverished and dry. Each spring, about 50g (2oz) of Growmore fertiliser worked into the surface of the soil around the base of each plant, will keep the plant from deteriorating and will also help to prevent yellowing or premature discolouration of the leaves. After application the fertiliser must be watered in thoroughly so that the soil is soaked to at least 30cm (1ft) below the surface.

In addition a layer of well rotted farmyard manure, spread around the base of the plants in spring will serve a twofold purpose in enriching the soil and acting as a moisture retaining mulch. A layer of peat will also help to keep the roots cool and conserve moisture but, unlike manure, will not provide the plant with nutrients.

Plants growing in large tubs or containers will need more regular feeding than those growing in the open ground. Starting two to three months after potting, apply a liquid feed with a high potassium content, such as a tomato fertiliser, once a week during the growing period. After the first season of growth an alternative to continual liquid feeding is, each spring, to work in about 25g (1oz.) of John Innes Base Fertiliser or Growmore Fertiliser into the top few inches of soil. However, as this will only suffice for two to three months at the most, liquid feeding will need to be started from about midsummer onwards.

Clematis montana rubra clambers to the highest point of this Hampshire cottage. This plant flowers during May & June and will grow facing any direction.

PROPAGATION

Cuttings

Although this method is used by professional nurserymen to propagate clematis it is not the ideal way for an amateur to increase stocks. Rooting conditions have to be very carefully controlled and some cultivars are very much more difficult to propagate than others. An internodal cutting is used taken from the soft young stems in May, June or July. The cutting is prepared by severing the stem just above a pair of leaves, removing one of the leaves and then trimming the cutting so that about 4cm (1.5in) of stem remains below the leaf node. See figure 7. The cuttings are planted in a seed sowing compost and kept in a warm humid situation in a shaded glasshouse. Some cuttings such as those from the species will root fairly easily but the large flowered hybrids are very much more difficult.

Layering

This technique is preferred by amateur growers as it is fairly certain to succeed. A 10-15cm (4-6in.) flowerpot is filled with John Innes No.1 potting compost and sunk into the ground up to its rim and about 30-45cm. (12-18in.) away from the main plant. A young shoot is carefully bent downwards and where it touches the soil in the pot the stem should be slit upwards from below a node to just above the node. See figure 8. The cut surface of the stem should be planted just under the surface of the soil and kept in place with a clip made out of bent wire. A small piece of slate or a flat stone is placed over the area to keep the soil surface cool and moist; the pot must not be allowed to dry out at any time. The following March the young plant can be severed from its parent and replanted elsewhere.

Propagation from seed

Seed can be collected from early flowering hybrids or species when ripe which should be in September or October. At this stage the seed heads are fluffy and break away easily from the flower stem. Remove the tails from the seeds and sow them immediately in a seed sowing compost. Cover them with about 0.25-0.5cm (1/8 to 1/4in.) of compost, water in and place in a cold frame until germination takes place. The seedlings may appear erratically and some may take at least six months to germinate. Providing that they have not received pollen from another, different clematis, species will come true from seed. However this is not the case with the large flowered hybrids; they have a complex ancestry and flower colours of the seedlings can be varied and quite unlike the parents.

Root division

The herbaceous species *C. integrifolia, davidiana* etc. can be divided in the same manner as other perennial plants. They are dug up in January or February and the roots split into pieces by tearing them apart with a pair of garden forks placed back to back. Each piece must have a stem with a few good live buds and should be treated in the same way as any newly planted specimen bought from a garden centre or nursery.

Figure 7.
Taking a Cutting.

Figure 8.
Layering.

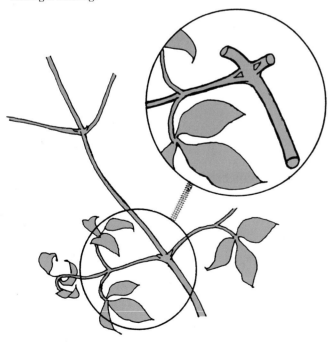

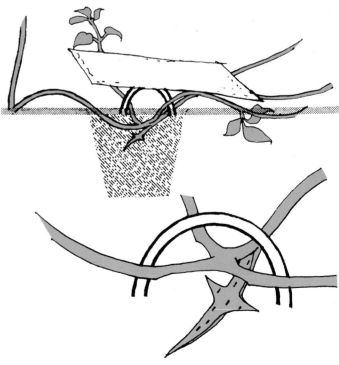

Cuttings are taken in May, June or July using the young stems and prepared in the manner shown. The cuttings can be dipped in hormone rooting powder before being inserted in compost up to the level of the leaf node.

This is a reliable way of propagating clematis. In sumer a young stem is slit half way through, just below a node. The cut surface can be dusted with hormone rooting powder before being covered with compost contained in a small flower pot sunk into the ground. The young plant will be ready to move into a new position by the following March.

Pests and Diseases

PESTS

Earwigs

These come out at night and eat holes in the leaves and flowers making the plants look unsightly. The pests can be trapped by the traditional method of catching them in a small inverted flower pot filled with straw hung or tied in contact with the foliage. Alternatively the plant can be sprayed with an insecticide containing gamma HCH or fenitrothion. Spray late in the evening so that the foliage remains wet until after dark when the earwigs are active.

Slugs and Snails

These can eat away the tips of the new stems that emerge close to the ground in the spring. Slug pellets or bait are quite effective as are the old fashioned beer traps. These consist of a shallow container filled with beer and sunk in the ground up to the rim. The pests are attracted by the beer and fall in and drown. A layer of ashes laid in a circle about two feet in diameter around the roots of the plant will also discourage these pests.

Snails in particular can climb considerable distances up walls, aided by the shelter given by the clematis. Examination of likely places will often uncover large clusters of snails that are responsible, like earwigs, for eating holes in the leaves and flowers well above ground level.

Aphids (Greenfly)

These pests occasionally attack clematis but are usually only a secondary colony from a more serious outbreak on a more favoured host situated nearby. Use one of the many proprietary sprays to eliminate the pest on the source of the outbreak as well as the clematis itself.

DISEASES

Clematis Wilt

This is probably the most important disease to affect clematis and unfortunately the full cause is not completely understood. Young plants are particularly affected, especially when they are making very rapid growth. Suddenly one or more of the stems will wilt completely as if they had been severed from the main plant. This wilted portion will not recover and should be cut away immediately and burnt or consigned to the rubbish bin. With luck new shoots will appear on the lower parts of the main stem and the disease will not re-occur but occasionally the plant will be lost completely. Planting in the manner described earlier, with two or three inches of the stem below ground, will give the plant a good chance of making a complete recovery. Affected plants can also be helped by spraying them with 'benlate' fungicide over the stems and leaves and using the same solution to soak thoroughly the immediate root area.

If persistent trouble is experienced with this disease try growing a different cultivar or planting one of the species, which as a group, are not normally susceptible to wilt. Before replanting change some of the soil, particularly the surface, on the site where a clematis has died.

Mildew

This forms a powdery grey deposit over the leaves and stems; some cultivars, such as the 'Jackmanii' hybrids are very much more prone to it than others. Spray affected plants with a fungicide containing carbendazim, mancozeb or benlate.

DISORDERS AND OTHER PROBLEMS

Leaf Discolouration

This is not always a cause for alarm as the lower leaves on some plants naturally turn brown quite early in the season. Some of the worst offenders are the pink and red hybrids; plenty of water and feeding will help to prevent this form of leaf discolouration. The 'Jackmanii' hybrids only produce flowers on the current seasons growth and can become bare and unsightly lower down. Correct initial planting and subsequent pruning should largely help to relieve this problem.

Pale and unhealthy leaves produced in the spring are probably caused by starvation, dryness, poor soil or a combination of these factors. Feed the plants with a fertiliser containing a high potassium content such as a tomato fertiliser and keep them well watered. If a clematis has been planted for less than three years it may not have had time to fully establish itself. Sometimes the large flowered hybrids may take up to five years before the roots penetrate to their maximum extent and the plants reach their full potential.

Some clematis are notorious for misbehaving in their early years but they usually settle down and become one of the garden's main attractions.

Luckily clematis are not particularly prone to disease but the average grower would be fortunate not to encounter some of the problems outlined in this section.

Sources of Supply

Most large garden centres now stock quite a wide range of containerised clematis for planting during most months of the year. However because they grow rapidly in the summer and quickly become entangled with each other stocks are usually kept to a minimum at this time. The more unusual kinds may not be stocked by every garden centre but they can usually be obtained from specialist nurseries. Two long established suppliers are listed below.

Fisk's Clematis Nursery,
Westleton, Nr. Saxmundham,
Suffolk. IP17 3AJ.
Tel: 072873 263.

Treasures of Tenbury Ltd.,
Burford House,
Tenbury Wells,
Worcestershire. WR15 8HQ.
Tel: 0584 81077.

Species, Cultivars and Varieties

The following illustrations show flowers which are typical examples of each cultivar. The colours are as accurate as modern developments in film and printing technology allow. Clematis flower colours can vary due to differences in soils, feeding and aspect. The change in colour between a newly opened flower and an old one is often very great, always fading with age.

The maximum heights and flowering periods quoted are averages from figures quoted by various growers throughout the British Isles. They are obviously only for rough guidance and must be interpreted with reference to the growers own situation and climatic conditions.

DEFINITION OF FLOWER SIZES
Small Up to 10cm (4in)
Medium 10-15cm (4 to 6in)
Large 15-20cm (6 to 8in)
Extra Large 20-25cm (8 to 10in)

'ALICE FISK'
Superb pale blue flowers with wavy petal edges and brown stamens. Introduced in 1967.
Flowering Period May, June & September.
Flower Size Large.
Planting Position Any.
Maximum Height 2-2.5m (6-8ft).
Pruning Required Tidy up plant in February.

alpina **'RUBY'**
A light purple-pink variety. Sometimes produces a few flowers during the summer months.
Flowering Period April & May.
Flower Size Small.
Planting Position Any.
Maximum Height 2.0-3.0m (6-10ft).
Pruning Required Tidy up plant in May or June.

'ALLANAH'
One colour ruby red. The sepals are spaced giving the flowers a pronounced wheel shape. Introduced in 1984.
Flowering Period June to September.
Flower Size Large.
Planting Position Not facing north.
Maximum Height 2-2.5m (6-8ft).
Pruning Required Hard, down to lowest 2 or 3 buds in February.

alpina **'WILLY'**
White lantern shaped flowers flushed with pinkish-mauve at the base of the sepals. Very free flowering.
Flowering Period April & May.
Flower Size Small.
Planting Position Any.
Maximum Height 2.0-3.0m (6-10ft).
Pruning Required Tidy up plant in May or June.

alpina
Light blue lantern like flowers; revels in a cool position. This is a member of a group that is native to the Alps and China. Fluffy seed heads are produced after flowering.
Flowering Period April & May.
Flower Size Small.
Planting Position Any, likes facing north.
Maximum Height 2.0-3.0m (6-10ft).
Pruning Required Tidy up plant in May or June.

'ASAO'
Deep pink, slightly darker around the petal edges. A new cultivar from Japan.
Flowering Period May, June & September.
Flower Size Large.
Planting Position Any.
Maximum Height 2.5-3.0m (8-10ft).
Pruning Required Tidy up plant in February.

'BARBARA DIBLEY'
Deep red with darker bars and red anthers. Best grown out of strong sunlight; attractive seed heads are formed after flowering.
Flowering Period May & June, August & September.
Flower Size Large.
Planting Position Preferably not facing north or south.
Maximum Height 2.5-3.0m (8-10ft).
Pruning Required Tidy up plant in February.

'COMTESSE DE BOUCHARD'
Mauve-pink. Vigorous and very free flowering. Reliable, recommended as good late flowering cultivar.
Flowering Period June to early September.
Flower Size Medium to large.
Planting Position Any.
Maximum Height 4m (13ft).
Pruning Required Hard, down to lowest 2 or 3 buds in February.

'BARBARA JACKMAN'
Pale blue-mauve sepals with deep red bars and beautiful yellow anthers. Suitable for cut flowers, best colour produced out of strong sunlight.
Flowering Period May, June & September.
Flower Size Medium to large.
Planting Position Not facing south.
Maximum Height 2.5-3.0m (8-10ft).
Pruning Required Tidy up plant in February.

'CRIMSON KING'
Light crimson with brownish stamens. A strikingly clear colour and very free flowering.
Flowering Period June to September.
Flower Size Large.
Planting Position Not facing north.
Maximum Height 2.5-3.0m (8-10ft).
Pruning Required Light after flowering.

calycina (syn.*balearica*)
Ferny evergreen leaves, yellow flowers with red spots on the inside. Also called the Fern Leaved Clematis.
Flowering Period January to March.
Flower Size Small.
Planting Position Any, sheltered.
Maximum Height 3.0-6.0m (10-20ft).
Pruning Required Tidy up plant after flowering.

'C. W. DOWMAN'
White or pale pink flowers with a light mauve bar. Rather like a paler version of the very popular 'Nelly Moser'.
Flowering Period May & June.
Flower Size Large.
Planting Position Not facing south.
Maximum Height 2.5-3.5m (8-10ft).
Pruning Required Tidy up plant in February.

'CAPITAN THUILLEAUX'
(Souvenir de Capitaine Thuilleaux)
Deep pink bars on a near white background. Very striking; introduced in 1969 and best grown out of strong sunlight to prevent the flowers from being bleached.
Flowering Period May, June & September.
Flower Size Large.
Planting Position Any.
Maximum Height 2.5-3.0m (8-10ft).
Pruning Required Tidy up plant in February.

davidiana **'WYVALE'**
(Syn. heracleifolia ' Wyvale')
Mid blue; small clusters of bell shaped flowers. Scented.
Flowering Period August to September.
Flower Size Small. **Planting Position** Any. A herbaceous plant.
Maximum Height 0.75m (30in).
Pruning Required Down to lowest buds in February or March.

'DAWN'
(Syn. 'Aurora')
Pearly white, tinged greyish
mauve when young.
Reddish-brown anthers. Good
as a cut flower; attractive seed
heads produced a few weeks
after flowering.
Flowering Period May &
June.
Flower Size Large.
Planting Position Facing west
or east.
Maximum Height 2-2.5m
(6-8ft).
Pruning Required Tidy up
plant in February.

'EDITH'
Pure white with red anthers. A
seedling from 'Mrs
Cholmondeley' first introduced
in 1974.
Flowering Period May &
June, August & September.
Flower Size Large.
Planting Position Any.
Maximum Height 3m (10ft).
Pruning Required Tidy up
plant in February.

'DANIEL DERONDA'
Deep blue with lighter
markings down the centre of
each sepal. Semi-double or
single flowers in spring, single
in autumn. A robust cultivar,
highly recommended.
Flowering Period May &
June, August & September.
Flower Size Extra large or
large.
Planting Position Preferably
not facing north.
Maximum Height 2.5-3.0m
(8-10ft).
Pruning Required Tidy up
plant in February.

'ELSA SPATH'
(Syn. 'Xerxes')
Deep blue with red anthers,
very free flowering. One of the
best clematis available,
strongly recommended.
Flowering Period May to
September.
Flower Size Large.
Planting Position Not facing
north.
Maximum Height 2-3m
(6-10ft).
Pruning Required Lightly in
February.

'DR. RUPPEL'
Pale pink with a wide red bar.
Very striking and exceptionally
free flowering. Introduced in
1975 and could become one of
the most popular of clematis.
Highly recommended.
Flowering Period May, June
& September.
Flower Size Large.
Planting Position Any.
Maximum Height 2.5-3.0m
(8-10ft).
Pruning Required Tidy up
plant in February.

x eriostemon
Nodding deep blue flowers. A
cross between *C. viticella* and
C. integrifolia.
Flowering Period July to
October.
Flower Size Small.
Planting Position Not facing
north.
Maximum Height 3-5m
(10-16ft).
Pruning Required Hard, to
lowest 2 or 3 buds in February

**'DUCHESS OF
EDINBURGH'**
Fully double, rosette shaped,
white flowers. Many of the
sepals are strongly tinged with
green and the flower seems to
gradually merge with the
foliage. For those who like
something unusual.
Flowering Period June to
August.
Flower Size Medium.
Planting Position Preferably
not facing north.
Maximum Height 2-3m
(6-10ft).
Pruning Required Tidy up
plant in February.

'ERNEST MARKHAM'
One toned deep glowing red.
Flowering Period July to
September or October.
Flower Size Medium.
Planting Position Not facing
north.
Maximum Height 3-5m
(10-16ft).
Pruning Required Hard, down
to lowest 2 or 3 buds in
February.

12

'FAIR ROSAMUND'
White, sometimes with a faint pink bar. Slightly scented. An old established cultivar best grown out of strong sunlight.
Flowering Period May & June.
Flower Size Medium to large.
Planting Position Preferably not facing north or south.
Maximum Height 2-3m (6-10ft).
Pruning Required Tidy up plant in February.

'GENERAL SIKORSKI'
Mid blue flowers with crinkled edges to the sepals and golden stamens. Introduced in 1980.
Flowering Period June to September.
Flower Size Large.
Planting Position Not facing north.
Maximum Height 2.5-3.0m (8-10ft).
Pruning Required Tidy up plant in February.

florida bicolor
(Syn.'Sieboldii') An unusual and rather tender plant with cream sepals and purple sepaloids.
Flowering Period June to September.
Flower Size Medium.
Planting Position Sheltered, against a wall facing south or in glasshouse.
Maximum Height 2.0-2.5m (6-8ft).
Pruning Required Remove all dead stems in February or March.

'GIPSY QUEEN'
Deep violet-purple velvety flowers with dark red anthers. Very free flowering; one of the best of this type.
Flowering Period July to October.
Flower Size Medium to large.
Planting Position Preferably not facing north.
Maximum Height 3-5m (10-16ft).
Pruning Required Hard, down to lowest 2 or 3 buds in February.

florida alba plena
Creamy yellow double flowers with a green centre.
Flowering Period June to September.
Flower Size Medium.
Planting Position Very sheltered against a wall facing south or in glasshouse.
Maximum Height 2m (6ft).
Pruning Required Remove all dead stems in February or March.

'H. F. YOUNG'
Wedgewood blue with golden stamens. Very free flowering. An absolutely stunning plant that should be in every garden, very highly recommended.
Flowering Period May & June, August & September.
Flower Size Large.
Planting Position Preferably not facing north.
Maximum Height 2.5-3.0m (8-10ft).
Pruning Required Tidy up plant in February.

'FOUR STAR'
Pale lavender with a deeper bar. A relatively new introduction from the USA.
Flowering Period May, June & September.
Flower Size Large.**Planting Position** Any.
Maximum Height 2.5-3.0m (8-10ft).
Pruning Required Tidy up plant in February.

integrifolia
Deep blue nodding flowers.
Flowering Period June to September.
Flower Size Small.
Planting Position Any, in the herbaceous border.
Maximum Height 0.7m (28in).
Pruning Required Remove all dead stems in February.

integrifolia 'DURANDII'
Deep blue bell shaped flowers, not a self clinging plant.
Flowering Period June to September.
Flower Size Small.
Planting Position Any. Needs tying to a support if grown in the herbaceous border.
Maximum Height 2.0-2.5m (6-8ft).
Pruning Required Down to lowest 2 or 3 buds in February or March.

'LADY NORTHCLIFFE'
Wedgewood blue flowers with white anthers.Compact growth, suitable for a small garden or container growing.
Flowering Period June to September.
Flower Size Medium.
Planting Position Preferably not facing north.
Maximum Height 2.0-2.5m (6-8ft).
Pruning Required Tidy up plant in February.

'JACKMANII RUBRA'
Deep red form with semi-double, double or single flowers.
Flowering Period June to September continuously.
Flower Size Medium.
Planting Position Any.
Maximum Height 3-5m (10-16ft).
Pruning Required Hard, down to lowest 2 or 3 buds in February.

'LASURSTERN'
Deep blue with cream stamens.
Flowering Period May & June, August & September.
Flower Size Large or extra large.
Planting Position Preferably not facing north.
Maximum Height 2.5-3.0m (8-10ft).
Pruning Required Tidy up plant after flowering

'JOAN PICTON'
The white central bars are broadly edged with soft lilac. A beautiful and unusual colour combination.
Flowering Period May, June & September.
Flower Size Large.
Planting Position Any.
Maximum Height 2.5-3.0m (8-10ft).
Pruning Required Tidy up plant in February.

'LINCOLN STAR'
Aptly named star shaped flower. Raspberry pink with pale edges. The early flowers are very much deeper and a more one toned raspberry red.
Flowering Period May & June, August & September.
Flower Size Large.
Planting Position Preferably not facing south.
Maximum Height 2.5-3.0m (8-10ft).
Pruning Required Tidy up plant in February.

'KATHLEEN WHEELER'
A plum-mauve colour with golden yellow stamens. Suitable for cut flowers.
Flowering Period June & September.
Flower Size Extra Large.
Planting Position Any.
Maximum Height 2.5-3.0m (8-10ft).
Pruning Required Tidy up plant in February.

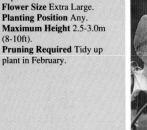

'LORD NEVILL'
Intense dark blue flowers with wavy sepal edges and purple-red anthers.
Flowering Period May & June, August & September.
Flower Size Large.
Planting Position Prefers facing south or west.
Maximum Height 2.5-3.0m (8-10ft).
Pruning Required Tidy up plant in February.

'LOUISE ROWE'
A very attractive pale mauve flower. Produces masses of double semi-double or single flowers all at the same time. Introduced in 1984.
Flowering Period June, July & September.
Flower Size Large.
Planting Position Not facing north.
Maximum Height 2-2.5m (6-8ft).
Pruning Required Tidy up plant in February.

'MARGARET HUNT'
An unusual shade of dusky pink, Exceptionally free flowering all summer. Introduced in 1969.
Flowering Period June to September.
Flower Size Medium.
Planting Position Any.
Maximum Height 3.5-6.0m (11-20ft).
Pruning Required Hard, down to lowest 2 or 3 buds in February.

macropetala
Freely produced semi-double mid blue flowers followed by fluffy seed heads.
Flowering Period April & May.
Flower Size Small.
Planting Position Any.
Maximum Height 2.5-3.0m (8-10ft).
Pruning Required Tidy up plant after flowering.

'MISS BATEMAN'
Creamy-white with attractive reddish stamens. Free flowering and with a compact habit.
Flowering Period May to June, occasionally in September.
Flower Size Medium.
Planting Position Preferably not facing north.
Maximum Height 2-2.5m (6-8ft).
Pruning Required Tidy up plant in February.

macropetala
'MARKHAMII' ('Markhams Pink') A pink version of the above species.
Flowering Period April & May.
Flower Size Small.
Planting Position Any.
Maximum Height 2.5-3.0m (8-10ft).
Pruning Required Tidy up plant after flowering.

'MISS CHOLMONDELEY'
A pale blue cultivar with broad sepals and brownish anthers. Rather open "gappy" flowers but they are produced in great profusion.
Flowering Period May to September.
Flower Size Large or extra large.
Planting Position Any.
Maximum Height 3-5m (10-16ft).
Pruning Required Tidy up plant in February.

MADAME EDOUARD ANDRE'
Dusky red pointed sepals and yellow anthers.
Flowering Period June to September.
Flower Size Medium.
Planting Position Any.
Maximum Height 2.0-3.0m (6-10ft).
Pruning Required Hard, down to lowest 2 or 3 buds in February.

montana **'ELIZABETH'**
Masses of pale pink, scented flowers.
Flowering Period May & June.
Flower Size Small.
Planting Position Any.
Maximum Height 6-9m (20-30ft).
Pruning Required Tidy up plant after flowering.

montana 'MAYLEEN'
Large mid pink with pronounced yellow stamens.
Flowering Period May & June.
Flower Size Small.
Planting Position Any.
Maximum Height 6-9m (20-30ft).
Pruning Required Tidy up plant after flowering.

'MRS SPENCER CASTLE'
Pale mauve-pink with golden stamens. Semi-double flowers in the spring, single flowers in autumn.
Flowering Period May, June & September.
Flower Size Medium.
Planting Position Any.
Maximum Height 3.0-5.0m (10-16ft).
Pruning Required Tidy up plant in February.

montana 'TETRAROSE'
Deep pink flowers with straw coloured stamens and bronzed foliage.
Flowering Period May & June.
Flower Size Small but largest of the group.
Planting Position Any.
Maximum Height 5m (15ft).
Pruning Required Tidy up plant after flowering.

'MYOJO'
Velvety red with deeper bar. Cream stamens. Newly introduced from Japan.
Flowering Period May, June & September.
Flower Size Large.
Planting Position Any.
Maximum Height 2.5-3.0m (8-10ft).
Pruning Required Tidy up plant in February.

'MRS N. THOMPSON'
Deep blue with a bright scarlet bar. Strikingly colourful and will always command attention wherever grown.
Flowering Period May & June, August & September.
Flower Size Medium to large.
Planting Position Preferably west or east.
Maximum Height 2.5-3.0m (8-10ft).
Pruning Required Tidy up plant in February.

'NIOBE'
Deepest red with yellow anthers. Despite its colour it will stand full sunshine well and is regarded as one of the best deep red clematis available. Raised in Poland.
Flowering Period June to September.
Flower Size Large.
Planting Position Preferably not facing north.
Maximum Height 2.5-3.0m (8-10ft).
Pruning Required Hard, down to lowest 2 or 3 buds in February.

'MRS P. B. TRUAX'
Mid blue flowers with yellow stamens. Fairly compact habit.
Flowering Period May & June, occasionally in September.
Flower Size Medium to large.
Planting Position Not facing north.
Maximum Height 2.0-3.0m (6-10ft).
Pruning Required Tidy up plant in February.

orientalis
Deep yellow or yellowish-orange bell shaped flowers; very thick sepals.
Flowering Period July to October.
Flower Size Small.
Planting Position Not facing north.
Maximum Height 3-6m (10-20ft).
Pruning Required Hard, to about 4 to 5 buds in February.

'PINK FANTASY'
Pale pink with a narrow deep red bar. Introduced in 1975.
Flowering Period June to September.
Flower Size Large.
Planting Position Not facing north.
Maximum Height 2.5-3.0m (8-10ft).
Pruning Required Hard, down to lowest 2 or 3 buds in February.

'ROUGE CARDINAL'
Deep velvety crimson with reddish-brown stamens.
Flowering Period June to September.
Flower Size Medium to large.
Planting Position Preferably not facing north.
Maximum Height 2.5m (8ft).
Pruning Required Hard, down to lowest 2 or 3 buds in February.

'PRINCE CHARLES'
Pale mauve-blue flowers produced in abundance; a very compact plant and ideal for the small garden. Introduced to the U.K. in 1986 from New Zealand.
Flowering Period June to September.
Flower Size Medium
Planting Position Not facing north.
Maximum Height 1.2-2m (4-6ft).
Pruning Required Hard, to lowest 2 or 3 buds in February.

'SILVER MOON'
Pale greyish lavender with yellow stamens. Attractive and unusual.
Flowering Period June to September.
Flower Size Large.
Planting Position Any.
Maximum Height 2.5-3.0m (8-10ft).
Pruning Required Tidy up or lightly prune in February.

'RAMONA'
Lavender blue with dark stamens.
Flowering Period June to September.
Flower Size Large.
Planting Position Any.
Maximum Height 3.0-5.0m (10-16ft).
Pruning Required Tidy up or prune lightly in February.

'SNOW QUEEN'
Pearly white with a hint of greenish-grey. A new cultivar (introduced in 1984) with an aristocratic appearance.
Flowering Period May, June & September.
Flower Size Large.
Planting Position Not facing north.
Maximum Height 2.0-2.5m (6-8ft).
Pruning Required Tidy up plant in February.

rehderiana
Clusters of tiny bell shaped, cowslip scented flowers.
Flowering Period August to October.
Flower Size Small.
Planting Position Not facing north.
Maximum Height 3.0-6.0m (10-20ft).
Pruning Required Tidy up plant after flowering.

'STAR OF INDIA'
Deep purple-blue flowers with a carmine bar. Very free flowering.
Flowering Period End June to early September.
Flower Size Medium.
Planting Position Any.
Maximum Height 3-5m (10-16ft).
Pruning Required Hard, down to lowest 2 or 3 buds in February.

'SYLVIA DENNY'
Pure white double flowers, golden stamens. Introduced in 1983. A very beautiful cultivar but can be difficult to propagate from cuttings. Like all the double flowered hybrids best grown through a shrub for extra support.
Flowering Period May, June & September.
Flower Size Large
Planting Position Not facing north.
Maximum Height 2.0-2.5m (6-8ft).
Pruning Required Tidy up plant in February.

'TWILIGHT'
Unusual dusky mauve with yellow anthers.
Flowering Period Continuously July to October.
Flower Size Large.
Planting Position Not facing north.
Maximum Height 2.5-3.0m (8-10ft).
Pruning Required Hard, down to lowest 2 or 3 buds in February.

tangutica **'GRAVETYE'**
Lantern shaped deep yellow flowers followed by masses of feathery seed heads.
Flowering Period August & September
Flower Size Small.
Planting Position Preferably not facing north.
Maximum Height 3-5m (10-16ft).
Pruning Required Light, after flowering.

'VICTORIA'
Light purple fading to a rosy-mauve, exceptionally free flowering and ideal for growing through trees.
Flowering Period End June to September.
Flower Size Medium.
Planting Position Any.
Maximum Height 3-5m (10-16ft).
Pruning Required Hard, down to lowest 2 or 3 buds in February.

texensis
'GRAVETYE BEAUTY'
Ruby-red tulip like flowers.
Flowering Period July to October.
Flower Size Small.
Planting Position Preferably not facing north.
Maximum Height 2.0-2.5m (6-8ft).
Pruning Required Hard, to lowest 2 or 3 buds in February.

'VILLE DE LYON'
Beautiful, rounded, carmine-red and crimson flowers. Must have a moist position or be kept well watered or the lower leaves will turn brown prematurely.
Flowering Period July to October.
Flower Size Large.
Planting Position Not facing north.
Maximum Height 2.5-3.0m (8-10ft).
Pruning Required Hard, down to lowest 2 or 3 buds in February.

'THE PRESIDENT'
Deep purple-blue. Exceptionally free flowering and reliable. One of the best of this colour, highly recommended.
Flowering Period May to September.
Flower Size Large.
Planting Position Any.
Maximum Height 2.5-3.0m (8-10ft).
Pruning Required Tidy up plant in February.

viticella
'ETOILE VIOLETTE'
Deep violet-purple with prominent golden stamens.
Flowering Period July to September.
Flower Size Medium.
Planting Position Preferably not facing north.
Maximum Height 2.5-3.5m (8-11ft).
Pruning Required Hard, to lowest 2 or 3 buds in February

viticella
'MADAME JULIA CORREVON'
Deep wine red recurving sepals.
Flowering Period Continuously from late June to September.
Flower Size Small.
Planting Position Any.
Maximum Height 2.0 -3.0m (6-10ft)
Pruning Required Hard, to lowest 2 or 3 buds in February.

'WARSAW NIKE'
An outstanding royal purple with golden anthers. Introduced to the U.K. from Poland in 1986.
Flowering Period June to September.
Flower Size Large.
Planting Position Not facing north.
Maximum Height 2.5-3.0m (8-10ft).
Pruning Required Hard, down to lowest 2 or 3 buds in February.

'VOLUCEAU'
Deep red with yellow anthers.
Flowering Period June to September.
Flower Size Medium.
Planting Position Not facing north.
Maximum Height 2.5-3.0m (8-10ft).
Pruning Required Hard, down to lowest 2 or 3 buds in February.

'WILLIAM KENNETT'
Pale lavender blue with red-purple stamens. The sepal edges are crimped and wavy. An old favourite.
Flowering Period June to early September.
Flower Size Large.
Planting Position Any.
Maximum Height 3.5-6.0m (11-20ft).
Pruning Required Tidy up or prune lightly in February.

'VYVYAN PENNELL'
Lavender and violet-mauve, rather variable colouration. Double or semi-double flowers. One of the best double flowered clematis.
Flowering Period May, June & September.
Flower Size Large.
Planting Position Not facing north.
Maximum Height 2.5-3.0m (8-10ft).
Pruning Required Tidy up plant in February.

SEEDHEADS
The seedheads of many clematis are highly decorative and ornamental. The example depicted here is the seedhead of 'Dawn' and is typical of a number of the cultivars and species. They can be either left on the plants or cut and used as attractive indoor decorations.

'WADA'S PRIMROSE'
Creamy white with a greenish bar. Even in shade the colour is disappointing. 'Yellow Queen', introduced in 1968 has similar characteristics.
Flowering Period May & June.
Flower Size Large.
Planting Position Any. Best colour facing north.
Maximum Height 3-5m (10-16ft).
Pruning Required Tidy up plant in February.

STAMENS AND ANTHERS
The deep red-purple pollen bearing anthers can be seen clearly in this enlargement of a flower of 'William Kennett'. The anthers are held on whitish filaments; the anthers and filaments together are called stamens. Clematis display their stamens very prominently and therefore are a very important and often colourful feature of the flowers.

Additional Descriptions
(Not Illustrated)

alpina 'COLUMBINE'
Pale blue, small nodding lantern shaped flowers.
Flowering Period April.
Flower Size Small.
Planting Position Any.
Maximum Height 2.5-3.0m (8-10ft).
Pruning Required Tidy up plant in May.

alpina 'FRANCES RIVIS'
Mid blue lantern shaped flowers.
Flowering Period April & May.
Flower Size Small.
Planting Position Any.
Maximum Height 2.0-2.5m (6-8ft).
Pruning Required Tidy up plant in May or June.

alpina 'PAMELA JACKMAN'
Mid blue lantern shaped flowers followed by attractive seed heads.
Flowering Period April.
Flower Size Small
Planting Position Any.
Maximum Height 2.5-3.0m (8-10ft).
Pruning Required Tidy up plant in May.

alpina 'WHITE MOTH'
Attractive white double flowers.
Flowering Period April.
Flower Size Small.
Planting Position Any.
Maximum Height 2.0-3.0m (6-10ft).
Pruning Required Tidy up plant in May.

armandii
Cluster of white, slightly scented flowers. Large glossy evergreen leaves. Rather tender.
Flowering Period March & April.
Flower Size Small.
Planting Position Sheltered, south or west facing.
Maximum Height 3-6m (10-20ft).
Pruning Required Tidy up plant in May.

'ASCOTIENSIS'
Long, pointed blue sepals, green stamens.
Flowering Period Continuously July to September.
Flower Size Large.
Planting Position Any.
Maximum Height 2.5-3.0m (8-10ft)
Pruning Required Hard, to lowest 2 or 3 buds in February.

'BEAUTY OF WORCESTER'
A pale lavender blue cultivar with fully double flowers in spring and single in autumn.
Flowering Period May & June & September.
Flower Size Large.
Planting Position Preferably not facing north.
Maximum Height 2.5-3.0m (8-10ft)
Pruning Required Tidy up plant in February.

'BEES JUBILEE'
Mauve-pink with carmine bars. Similar but superior to 'Nelly Moser'.
Flowering Period May & June, August or September.
Flower Size Large.
Planting Position Preferably not facing south.
Maximum Height 2.5-3.0m (8-10ft).
Pruning Required Tidy up plant in February.

'BELLE NANTAISE'
A lavender-blue flower with white stamens.
Flowering Period June to September.
Flower Size Extra large.
Planting Position Any.
Maximum Height 2.5-3.0m (8-10ft).
Pruning Required Tidy up or light pruning in February.

'BELLE OF WOKING'
Silvery-grey double flowers that become single in autumn.
Flowering Period May & June, August or September.
Flower Size Medium.
Planting Position Any.
Maximum Height 2.5-3.0m (8-10ft).
Pruning Required Tidy up plant in February.

'CHARISSIMA'
Cerise-pink with a deeper bar and veining.
Flowering Period June to September.
Flower Size Extra large.
Planting Position Any.
Maximum Height 2.5-3.0m (8-10ft).
Pruning Required Tidy up plant in February.

chrysocoma
Light pink flowers with yellow stamens. Downy young growth.
Flowering Period May & June.
Flower Size Small.
Planting Position Any.
Maximum Height 6m (20ft) or more.
Pruning Required Tidy up plant in July.

'COUNTESS OF LOVELACE'
Good lilac-blue double flowers on the old wood, single on new.
Flowering Period June to September.
Flower Size Large.
Planting Position Any.
Maximum Height 2.5-3.0m (8-10ft).
Pruning Required Tidy up plant in February.

'DUCHESS OF SUTHERLAND'
Carmine-red with a lighter bar, creamy yellow stamens.
Flowering Period June to August or September.
Flower Size Medium to large.
Planting Position Preferably not facing north.
Maximum Height 2.5-3.0m (8-10ft).
Pruning Required Tidy up or prune lightly in February.

flammula
Masses of small, white, scented star shaped flowers followed by silvery seed heads.
Flowering Period August to October.
Flower Size Small.
Planting Position Preferably not facing north.
Maximum Height 5-6m (16-20ft).
Pruning Required Tidy up plant in February.

'HAGLEY HYBRID'
A very free flowering pink cultivar.
Flowering Period Late June to August or September.
Flower Size Medium.
Planting Position Preferably not south.
Maximum Height 2.0-2.5m (6-8ft).
Pruning Required Hard, to lowest 2 or 3 buds in February.

'HENRYI'
Almost pure creamy white with brown anthers.
Flowering Period June to August or September.
Flower Size Large or extra large.
Planting Position Any.
Maximum Height 3-5m (10-16ft).
Pruning Required Tidy up or lightly prune in February.

'HULDINE'
Pearly white, very vigorous and free flowering.
Flowering Period Late June to September or October.
Flower Size Small to medium.
Planting Position Preferably not facing north.
Maximum Height 3.5-6.0m (12-20ft).
Pruning Required Hard, to lowest 2 or 3 buds in February.

'JACKMANII'
The most popular purple cultivar; green stamens.
Flowering Period Continuously June to September.
Flower Size Medium to large.
Planting Position Any.
Maximum Height 3.5-6.0m (11-20ft).
Pruning Required Hard, to lowest 2 or 3 buds in February.

'JACKMANII ALBA'
An off white form that sometimes produces semi-double flowers on the old wood.
Flowering Period Late June to August or September.
Flower Size Medium to large.
Planting Position Any.
Maximum Height 2.5-3.0m (8-10ft).
Pruning Required Hard, to lowest 2 or 3 buds in February.

'JACKMANII SUPERBA'
Deep purple sepals, broader than 'Jackmanii'. Green stamens. Very popular.
Flowering Period June or July to August or September.
Flower Size Large.
Planting Position Any.
Maximum Height 3-5m (10-16ft).
Pruning Required Hard, to lowest 2 or 3 buds in February.

'JOHN PAUL II'
Broad, crinkled, creamy white sepals, tinged with pink particularly in late summer.
Flowering Period May & June, September.
Flower Size Medium.
Planting Position Any.
Maximum Height 3-5m (10-16ft).
Pruning Required Tidy up plant in February.

'JOHN WARREN'
Deep pink central bar and sepal edges on a greyish ground.
Flowering Period May & June, August or September.
Flower Size Large.
Planting Position Preferably not facing south.
Maximum Height 2.0-3.0m (6-10ft).
Pruning Required Tidy up plant in February.

jouiniana
Non clinging species with masses of pale blue flowers. Can be used as ground cover.
Flowering Period September & October.
Flower Size Small.
Planting Position Semi-herbaceous; not facing north.
Maximum Height 3-5m (10-16ft).
Pruning Required Hard, to lowest 2 or 3 buds in February.

'KATHLEEN DUNFORD'
Rich rosy-purple with golden yellow stamens. Semi-double flowers in spring, single in the autumn. An unusual cultivar with deep green foliage and compact growth.
Flowering Period May, June & September.
Flower Size Large.
Planting Position Any.
Maximum Height 2.5-3.0m (8-10ft).
Pruning Required Tidy up plant in February.

'LADY BETTY BALFOUR'
Purple-blue with yellow stamens. A late flowering cultivar.
Flowering Period Late August to October.
Flower Size Large.
Planting Position Preferably facing south.
Maximum Height 3.5-6.0m (11-20ft).
Pruning Required Hard, to lowest 2 or 3 buds in February.

'LAWSONIANA'
Lavender-blue with a pinkish tint.
Flowering Period June to September.
Flower Size Extra large.
Planting Position Not facing north.
Maximum Height 3-5m (10-16ft).
Pruning Required Tidy up or prune lightly in February.

macropetala **'MAIDWELL HALL'**
The habit is similar to macropetela but the flower is a deeper shade of blue.
Flowering Period April and May.
Flower Size Small.
Planting Position Any.
Maximum Height 2.5-3m (8-10ft).
Pruning Required Tidy up plant in June.

macropetela **'WHITE SWAN'**
Double white nodding flowers.
Flowering Period April & May.
Flower Size Small.
Planting Position Any.
Maximum Height 2.5-3.0m (8-10ft).
Pruning Required Tidy up plant in June.

'MADAME BARON VEILLARD'
Lilac rose sepals, late flowering.
Flowering Period September and October.
Flower Size Medium
Planting Position Not facing north.
Maximum Height 3-5m (10-16ft).
Pruning Required Hard, to lowest 2 or 3 buds in February.

'MISS CRAWSHAY'
Mauvish-pink flowers, semi-double in spring, single in autumn.
Flowering Period June to September.
Flower Size Medium.
Planting Position Not facing north.
Maximum Height 2.5-3.0m (8-10ft).
Pruning Required Tidy up plant in February.

montana **'ALEXANDER'**
Creamy white, scented flowers with yellow stamens.
Flowering Period May and June.
Flower Size Small.
Planting Position Any.
Maximum Height 6m (20ft) plus.
Pruning Required Tidy up plant in July.

montana **'FREDA'**
Deep pink with a darker edge. Bronze leaves.
Flowering Period May & June.
Flower Size Small.
Planting Position Any.
Maximum Height 6m (20ft) plus.
Pruning Required Tidy up plant in July.

montana grandiflora
Fast growing species with masses of pure white flowers and yellow stamens. Best type for covering unsightly buildings etc.
Flowering Period May & June.
Flower Size Small.
Planting Position Any, happy facing north.
Maximum Height 12m (40ft).
Pruning Required None.

montana **'PICTON'S VARIETY'**
Deep satin pink flowers, some occasionally produced in the summer.
Flowering Period Usually May & June.
Flower Size Small.
Planting Position Any.
Maximum Height 5m (16ft).
Pruning Required Tidy up plant in July.

montana **'PINK PERFECTION'**
Medium pink flowers and yellow stamens.
Flowering Period May & June.
Flower Size Small.
Planting Position Any.
Maximum Height 9m (30ft).
Pruning Required Tidy up plant in July.

'PROTEUS'
Mauve-pink. Double or semi-double flowers on old wood, single on new.
Flowering Period May to June, August or September.
Flower Size Large.
Planting Position Preferably not facing north.
Maximum Height 2.5-3.0m (8-10ft).
Pruning Required Tidy up plant in February.

'RICHARD PENNELL'
Deep lavender with striking gold stamens.
Flowering Period May to June, August or September.
Flower Size Large.
Planting Position Any.
Maximum Height 2.5-3.0m (8-10ft).
Pruning Required Tidy up plant in February.

'SERENATA'
Very deep purple sepals, yellow stamens.
Flowering Period June to September.
Flower Size Medium to large.
Planting Position Preferably not facing north.
Maximum Height 2.5-3.5m (8-11ft).
Pruning Required Hard, to lowest 2 or 3 buds in February.

texensis **'DUCHESS OF ALBANY'**
Deep pink tulip shaped flowers.
Flowering Period July to September.
Flower Size Small
Planting Position Preferably not facing north.
Maximum Height 2.5-3.0m (8-10ft).
Pruning Required Hard, to lowest 2 or 3 buds in February.

texensis 'ETOILE ROSE'

Best viewed from below. The flowers are cerise-pink and bell shaped with silvery margins.
Flowering Period July to October.
Flower Size Small.
Planting Position Not facing north.
Maximum Height 2.5-3.0m (8-10ft).
Pruning Required Hard, to lowest 2 or 3 buds in February.

vedrariensis

Similar to the *montana* types but with downy foliage. Pink flowers.
Flowering Period May & June.
Flower Size Small.
Planting Position Any.
Maximum Height 6m (20ft).
Pruning Required Tidy up plant in July.

'VIOLET CHARM'.

The long pointed sepals are a rich violet–blue colour. Beige stamens.
Flowering Period June to September.
Flower size Large.
Planting Position Not facing north.
Maximum Height 2.0-2.5m (6-8ft).
Pruning Required Light pruning in February.

vitalba

Masses of star like creamy white flowers followed by attractive seed heads.
Flowering Period July to September.
Flower Size Small.
Planting Position Any.
Maximum Height 8m (26ft).
Pruning Required Hard, to lowest 2 or 3 buds in February.

viticella

Saucer shaped purple flowers that hang downwards; Vigorous.
Flowering Period July to September.
Flower Size Small.
Planting Position Not facing north.
Maximum Height 6-9m (20-30ft).
Pruning Required Hard, to lowest 2 or 3 buds in February.

viticella 'ABUNDANCE'

Mauve-red, freely produced flowers.
Flowering Period July to September.
Flower Size Small.
Planting Position Not facing north.
Maximum Height 3.5-6.0m (11-20ft).
Pruning Required Hard, to lowest 2 or 3 buds in February.

viticella 'ALBA LUXURIANS'

Creamy white, green tinted and twisted sepals.
Flowering Period July to September.
Flower Size Small.
Planting Position Not facing north.
Maximum Height 3.5-6.0m (11-20ft).
Pruning Required Hard, to lowest 2 or 3 buds in February.

viticella 'MARGOT KOSTER'

Deep pink-mauve freely produced flowers.
Flowering Period July to September.
Flower Size Small.
Planting Position Not facing north.
Maximum Height 3.5-6.0m (11-20ft).
Pruning Required Hard, to lowest 2 or 3 buds in February.

viticella purpurea plena elegans

A superb, double, free flowering form of C. viticella.
Flowering Period July to September.
Flower Size Small.
Planting Position Preferably not facing north.
Maximum Height 3.5-6.0m (11-20ft).
Pruning Required Hard, to lowest 2 or 3 buds in February.

viticella 'ROYAL VELOURS'

Deep purple with black anthers.
Flowering Period July to September.
Flower Size Small.
Planting Position Not facing north.
Maximum Height 3.5-6.0m (11-20ft).
Pruning Required Hard, to lowest 2 or 3 buds in February.

viticella 'RUBRA'

Deep wine red flowers, blackish-red stamens.
Flowering Period July to September.
Flower Size Small.
Planting Position Not facing north.
Maximum Height 3.5-6.0m (11-20ft).
Pruning Required Hard, to lowest 2 or 3 buds in February.

viticella 'VENOSA VIOLACEA'

Boat shaped sepals; deep purple with white veins.
Flowering Period June or July to September.
Flower Size Medium.
Planting Position Not facing north.
Maximum Height 3-5m (10-16ft).
Pruning Required Hard, to lowest 2 or 3 buds in February.

'WALTER PENNELL'

Deep pink flowers, tinged mauve. Double in spring, single in autumn.
Flowering Period May & June, September.
Flower Size Large.
Planting Position Any.
Maximum Height 2.5-3.0m (8-10ft).
Pruning Required Tidy up plant in February.

'W. E. GLADSTONE'

Pale blue flowers with red-purple stamens.
Flowering Period June to August or September.
Flower Size Extra large.
Planting Position Preferably not facing north.
Maximum Height 3-5m (10-16ft).
Pruning Required Tidy up or light pruning in February.

'WILHELMINA TULL'

Deep violet with a broad crimson bar and golden stamens. Similar to but said to be an improvement over the excellent 'Mrs N. Thompson'. Introduced in 1984.
Flowering Period May, June and September.
Flower Size Large.
Planting Position Not facing north.
Maximum Height 2.0-2.5m (6-8ft).
Pruning Required Tidy up plant in February.

'YELLOW QUEEN'

The colour can be a pale primrose yellow but the colour fades rapidly to an off white.
Flowering Period May and June.
Flower Size Large.
Planting Position West or east only.
Maximum Height 3m (10ft).
Pruning Required Tidy up plant in February.